Creative Chaos

Learning Lessons on Inclusion & Innovation
Making the Magic

Carnegie Mellon University
Entertainment Technology Center

LEARN WORK PLAY

Creative Chaos

Creative Chaos

Learning Lessons on Inclusion & Innovation | Making the Magic

Drew Davidson et al.

Carnegie Mellon: ETC Press
Pittsburgh

Copyright © by Drew Davidson et al. and ETC Press 2016
http://press.etc.cmu.edu/

ISBN: 978-1-365-49475-8 (Print)
ISBN: 978-1-365-49477-2 (eBook)
Library of Congress Control Number: 2016959339

TEXT: The text of this work is licensed under a Creative Commons Attribution-NonCommercial-NonDerivative 2.5 License (http://creativecommons.org/licenses/by-nc-nd/2.5/)

IMAGES: All images appearing in this work are property of the respective copyright owners, and are not released into the Creative Commons. The respective owners reserve all rights.

Contents

Preface & Acknowledgments — ix
Creative Chaos — xiii
Introduction — 1

I. OVERVIEW

1) On the ETC — 7

2) On Creativity — 11

3) On ETC Research — 16

4) On Creativity Research — 21

5) On ETC Curriculum — 25

II. LEARNING LESSONS

6) On Inclusion — 37

7) On Collegiality — 42

8) On Development — 47

9) On Context — 52

10) On Support — 57

11) On Challenge — 64

In Conclusion — 69
References — 73
About the Author(s) — 79
About the ETC Press — 82

- Preface & Acknowledgments

The idea for this book started when Laurie Weingart visited the Entertainment Technology Center (ETC). When she saw the ETC projects, she thought they would make for a great petri dish for a study on small group innovation. She proposed the idea to the ETC faculty, and we all agreed to collaborate. Working with two doctoral students, Kenneth Goh and Gergana Todorova, Laurie mounted a four-year study with the support of ETC faculty, staff and the students on project teams in order to figure out exactly how creative innovation happens. Once her data was collected and analyzed, Laurie, Kenneth and Gergana presented several research papers at academic conferences and also shared their results with the ETC. We believed these findings illustrate the "creative chaos" inherent in the dynamic process of collaborative design and development with interdisciplinary teams. We were excited not only to see how the data resonated with the faculty's qualitative understandings of how we were teaching, but also to find new ideas for how to improve. Working with Laurie and a new doctoral student, Anna Mayo, we dug into the data anew for more insights. Anita Woolley, a Tepper colleague, also shared insights from her studies on collective intelligence. We worked to update our curriculum based on the information, which included incorporating new ideas such as the playtesting workshops that Jodi Forlizzi helps us offer.

We wrote about "Creative Chaos" for the ETC website, and I included this topic in a lecture I give for the ETC Fundamentals class each year that all of our students take during their first semester. This in turn led to invitations to give this talk at various conferences and forums. To show the range of interest in this topic, here's a list of events and groups to date where I've shared this information: Meaningful Play, Dust or Magic, Education Summit at the Game Developers Conference, Design & Development Division Board for the Association for Educational Communications & Technology, The Michigan Department of Natural Resources, Bayer Innovation Symposium, Houghton Mifflin Harcourt Studios, Create Festival, Serious Play Conference, Thrival Innovation + Music Festival, Maker Educator Institute at the Pittsburgh Maker Faire, Games + Higher Education + National Impact, and Games for Change.

I adapted the talk for each event and audience. After one such talk, my colleague Mary Flanagan noted that capturing this information in a short book would be a useful resource to share. During the writing, Brad King helped focus this from a talk into a book. While I've been compiling all of this creative chaos together, I want to acknowledge that everyone mentioned above has contributed to this effort, sharing insights and expertise, reading drafts and helping shape the book overall. The process of creating this book exemplifies creative collaboration. We've all worked together and made this a much better book. Thanks to everyone involved.

Creative Chaos

- Learning Lessons on Inclusion & Innovation
- Making the Magic

Carnegie Mellon University
Entertainment Technology Center

Creativity is a wonderfully complex and chaotic process. Borrowing from Mark Twain, the difference between when the creative process goes well and when it doesn't is the difference between lightning and a lightning bug. At Carnegie Mellon University's Entertainment Technology Center (ETC), we often describe what we do as "creative chaos" in that it's not necessarily a process within which you ever have complete control. It's simultaneously exciting and exhausting, and trying to develop into a creative professional who can collaborate on interdisciplinary teams to regularly make inventive work with budgets, deadlines and clients is a challenging experience. And that's exactly what we work to teach at the ETC. In this short book we hope to share some of the applicable lessons we've been learning on how best to support creative work with diverse teams, and help them make the magic happen.

At the ETC, we balance educational goals, professional development and engaging experiences – or what we refer to as "learn, work, play." The ETC is the premiere professional graduate program for interactive entertainment as it is applied across a variety of fields. Founded in 1998, the ETC offers a unique two-year master's degree in entertainment technology (M.E.T.) that is jointly conferred by Carnegie Mellon University's School of Computer Science and the College of Fine Arts.

With an emphasis on leadership, innovation and communication, we create challenging experiences through which students learn how to collaborate, experiment and iterate solutions. We excel at the intersection of technology, art and design through interdisciplinary project work that focuses around a range of areas, spanning learning, health, training, social impact, civics, entertainment and more; and project teams develop games, animation, location-based installations, augmented reality, mobile devices, robotics, interactive performances, transmedia storytelling, etc. The ETC is simply different: We strive to design experiences that educate, engage and inspire.

Introduction

- Overview
- Learning Lessons

Carnegie Mellon University
Entertainment Technology Center

To explore creative chaos, this short book is organized into two major parts. Creative Chaos describes the dynamic process of collaborative design and development within interdisciplinary teams as they work to create something together. To articulate what this means, the first part provides an overview of the ETC and our research on how diversity, inclusion and innovation are related, and also how we support these three associated ideas through our project-based curriculum. The second part extrapolates from this to share some best practices from the lessons we've been learning about the creative process and how to make the most of the creative chaos.

I. Overview

I. Overview

- 1) On the ETC
- 2) On Creativity
- 3) On ETC Research
- 4) On Creativity Research
- 5) On ETC Curriculum

The first part on creative chaos is organized into the following five sections: the ETC, creativity, ETC research, creativity research, and ETC curriculum.

1) On the ETC

- ETC
- ETC Mission
- Art | Technology | Design
- Entertainment Technologies

ETC

Randy Pausch, one of the ETC's co-founders, liked to say that the ETC was the world's best playground (with an electric fence). He meant that creative work needed constraints. Doing innovative work is difficult when you're told that you can do whatever you want. Constraints come in the form of time or budget limits, and the goals of a project. These can be extrinsic exercises, like requiring a team to design a tabletop game, instead of a digital one. But mostly, they're intrinsic to the reality of the design and development process itself, as teams have to deal with the limited resources they have, the goals of the client, the needs of the user demographic, or many other possible constraints. These provide a context within which a project team can work.

Randy's statement also gets at the heart of the educational endeavor. In order to learn, students need to be challenged so that they can grow. And in order to do successful work, teams have to be willing to court failures on their way to the right solution. These all provide constraints within which creativity can flourish. If you want to do something extraordinary, you need boundaries between what is normal and what is special. And that's where the magic happens.

ETC MISSION

Providing leadership in education and applied research that combines technology and art, to explore learning, storytelling, innovation and entertainment, and to create experiences that educate, engage and inspire.

The ETC's mission is to provide leadership in education and applied research that combines technology and art, to explore learning, storytelling, innovation and entertainment, and to create experiences that educate, engage and inspire. The overall goal is to have interdisciplinary teams work together to create playable prototypes and working proofs of concept. This takes communication and collaboration across disciplines, so our curriculum is constructed to help support this process.

ART | TECHNOLOGY | DESIGN

The ETC was started seventeen years ago (as of the 2016/2017 academic year), co-founded out of CMU's College of Fine Arts and the School of Computer Science. Having a connection to both was intentional so that the program didn't skew too far towards just being technical or artistic. Instead, the ETC has an interdisciplinary basis that includes both and beyond.

ENTERTAINMENT TECHNOLOGIES

The strength of the ETC is the breadth of our focus, with an interest in entertainment technologies across the board. We explore games, animation, theme parks, museums, virtual/augmented/mixed reality, mobile, robotics, interactive performances, crossmedia and more. And we're interested in how all of these could be used in a variety of fields, like education and learning, health and medical, civic engagement, and of course, entertainment. This wide range serves as the foundation from which our team projects tackle various design and development challenges.

This range is also reflected in the careers of our alumni. We've found that about 50-60% go into the video game industry, about 10-15% go into Hollywood (animation studios and effects houses), 10-15% go into themed entertainment (theme parks, museums and science centers), 5-10% go into technology (e.g. Apple, Google, Microsoft), one or two students will go onto Ph.D. studies, and there's often one spin-off company formed around their student project work.

2) On Creativity

- Teaching Creativity
- Creative Production
- Creative Chaos
- Making Stuff
- Making the Magic

TEACHING CREATIVITY

The on-going challenge in trying to teach creativity is having to strike a delicate balance between giving direction, providing guidance and allowing enough freedom so that people can truly explore and engage with the creative process on their own. Striking this balance helps people learn that they can tap into their imaginations and focus together to create innovative work.

At the ETC we try to focus both on creativity as a skill that you can improve as well as a process that you go through in order to do creative work. This dual focus helps use balance between working to teach individuals how to tap their own creativity while also working to enable teams to do creative work together.

CREATIVE PRODUCTION

For the purpose of this book, when we talk about creativity the focus is more on creative production done on teams than on the work done by one person. Creativity is the design and development process an interdisciplinary team engages in as they work on a creative project together.

This process requires communication and collaboration because teams must have constructive discussions both internally and externally. This communication is a challenging process as the groups experience internal disagreements on the team, external issues with a client, or both, and more. Success requires support to help teams have constructive discussions as opposed to disruptive arguments. Good communication is the only way that a team can collaborate well together towards the goals of the project.

Leadership, in terms of team members taking responsibility for their roles and for the goals of the project as a whole, as opposed to wanting to be the boss of our colleagues, is needed to help a team focus on the vision and mission of a project. Management, in terms of coordinating a team's efforts to stay on time and on budget, is also important for a team in order to complete a project.

Overall, for creative production to happen in a constructive manner, teams have to develop and maintain trust and respect for each other. This happens across time and teams need to pay attention to make sure they have both in order to work well together on creative production.

CREATIVE CHAOS

Creative chaos is a term we use to try and encapsulate the creative production process, which is often full of ambiguous ideas about what you're trying to actually make. A large part of the challenge is working to help more clearly define the goals of a project. Also, in order to create something innovative a team has to take the risk of exploring new ideas and doing things that they haven't done before. This is also combined with the fact the results are invariably uncertain as a team can't know in advance that their ideas will actually meet the goals. This is done through rapid prototyping and iterative design that a team can work toward discovering what they need to make. This type of prototyping is an inherently flexible process in which a successful team needs to be comfortable taking risks and dealing with various unknowns as they iterate their way toward a good design that meets the goals of the project. The creative process is intrinsically chaotic: hence, creative chaos.

MAKING STUFF

The creative production process is also focused on actually making artifacts and the development of intellectual property. Our students tend to conflate their ideas with intellectual property. Ideas are often the easiest part and are not intellectual property. Implementing those ideas in order to make something is when you are creating intellectual property. When you're doing this with an interdisciplinary team, you're sharing the design and development as you create IP together. We often stress that what makes a team successful is that they come together to do the work that the project needs, as opposed to just doing what each person wants. This collaboration is when a team can really make something worthwhile.

MAKING THE MAGIC

Disney Imagineering's motto is "making the magic," which captures the creatively chaotic nature of actually making something innovative that really inspires and wows the audience when they experience what you've made. When doing creative work, teams need to consider what it means to be innovative. Innovation happens at the intersection of work that is new, useful and good quality. Just accomplishing one or two of the three isn't enough. True innovation requires all three.

To accomplish this, teams must try to follow a good design process of defining goals, and iterating on solutions. This is an applied research methodology as a team problem solves their way toward the project's goals. There are a plethora of methods to work through the design process, so we're not even going to try and capture all of them. Overall, good design requires critical creation in which a team carefully considers what they're making, and why they're making it, throughout the development process

3) On ETC Research

- How?
- CMU Tepper Study of ETC
- ETC Study Methods
- ETC Study Measures
- ETC Study Results
- Further ETC Data

HOW?

The big questions are how can teams succeed at doing creative work, and how can they do it across multiple projects and years? Also, how can you teach people to improve at doing innovative work?

CMU TEPPER STUDY OF ETC

Dr. Laurie Weingart, Senior Associate Dean of Education and Richard M. and Margaret S. Cyert Professor of Organizational Behavior and Theory in the Tepper School of Business at Carnegie Mellon University, thought that the ETC's semester-long interdisciplinary projects would make for a great study on how creative teams manage to do innovative work, or not.

In 2008, Laurie Weingart started a study with two of her doctoral students, Gergana Todorova and Kenneth Goh (who are now at the University of Miami and the University of Western Ontario respectively). They engaged in a four-year study of ETC projects to explore if and how expertise diversity translates into innovation. In other words, do more disciplinary diverse teams create more innovative work?

ETC STUDY METHODS

Between 2008-2011 they studied 60 ETC projects, surveying the project teams four times each semester (at the start, 1/4s, 1/2s and finals) collecting general demographic data along with information on the design process. They supplemented these surveys with interviews and direct observations of team meetings. They also had the faculty provide independent ratings on quality and innovativeness of the final prototypes that the teams delivered, as well as how useful, usable and desirable they were.

ETC STUDY MEASURES

After collecting all of the data, Laurie Weingart and colleagues examined communication and conflict within design process of projects. Additionally, they examined how leadership and coordination arose through the process while taking into account the faculty ratings on the quality and innovation of the final project deliverables.

ETC STUDY RESULTS

What they discovered was that teams with more expertise diversity had more conflict about tasks in the form of disagreements and debates. Instead of being detrimental to team performance, these disagreements and debates led to final deliverables that were rated to be more innovative, useful, usable, and desirable. In other words, diverse teams can have constructive conflict in the form of debates around the task, as opposed to personal arguments, and this type of more constructive conflict often leads to better innovation outcomes overall.

FURTHER ETC DATA

In 2014, another of Laurie Weingart's doctoral students, Anna Mayo, joined the Tepper School of Business research team and together with them began further analyzing the data to examine the effects of other variables in the design process. Early indications have shown that diversity matters, and to consider why diversity matters is important in order to get the most out of the potential that diverse teams can provide. They have also shown that expertise diversity can often lead to more constructive conflict that is helpful for innovation. In a similar way, gender diversity is associated with more innovation in that mixed gender teams are associated with a better exchange of ideas. However, other demographic differences, such as ethnic diversity, didn't seem to matter as directly for team functioning.

Analyses have also shown that experience can affect outcomes. Having people with some work experience (even just an internship) leads to better innovation as well as more learning. While this suggests more work experience is always beneficial, the research also shows that experience working with one another is not always positive; teams that have some familiarity with each other seem to work well, yet too much familiarity can be harmful. Other research on this topic suggests that newcomers and new collaborations can offer new and fresh ideas that facilitate creativity.

Interestingly, the type of project (client, research or pitch) doesn't seem to matter, nor does the size of the project teams, nor which project instructors a team has. However, in looking at leadership, being supportive and showing consideration for your teammates seems to be more important than focusing on initiating structure by assigning members to particular tasks and defining standards of performance.

Overall, the data suggest diversity is important, but constructive conflict and the exchange of ideas emerge as the key reasons why some teams were more innovative than others. Importantly, research on diversity shows that that the very act of valuing diversity has a positive impact, leading to those key collaborative processes that allow for diverse teams to make use of their different knowledge and perspectives. In this way, inclusion leads to innovation.

These insights have affirmed for us that in order to do innovative work, orchestrating support for interdisciplinary teams is important. This support starts with striking an interdisciplinary balance as we recruit each incoming class to include people from varied backgrounds. This balance leads into a first semester of study where we emphasize the value of diverse ideas and perspectives, as they collaborate with all of their new colleagues and also take improvisational acting together. Improv is one of the best ways we have found for people to learn how to creatively collaborate with each other. Throughout, the faculty and staff model supportive leadership, and we work to continually improve the design of our curriculum with this in mind. Our goal is to help teams be able to constructively collaborate and communicate through the creative design and development process.

4) On Creativity Research

- Granted
- Resonant Research
- Collective Intelligence

GRANTED

The study on the ETC was focused on CMU graduate students so people might question if the results are applicable in other situations and scenarios. We believe there are some lessons we've been learning that could be helpful for a variety of groups who are doing collaborative work together.

RESONANT RESEARCH

There is ample related research that resonates with the results of the study on the ETC but much of that is outside of the scope of this short book to try and reference all of the relevant studies. However, two fairly recent meta-studies clearly distill some related findings.

A report by the Association of Computing Machinery found that diverse teams have a greater potential for innovation. The caveat was that the effectiveness of diverse teams depended upon having a trusting and supportive culture. While there are challenges to developing trust, the collected studies reference known methods that can help address this effectively. A Scientific American report reviews decades of research that show socially diverse groups are more innovative. The reviewed research also shows that just interacting with people who are different from us makes us more creative, more diligent and harder-working, enabling group members to prepare better, to anticipate alternative viewpoints and to understand that reaching consensus takes effort. Both of these meta-studies illustrate the valuable effect diversity can have, and highlight the challenges and support needed to make it a positive impact.

COLLECTIVE INTELLIGENCE

Similarly, Dr. Anita Woolley, an Associate Professor of Organizational Behavior and Theory in the Tepper School of Business at CMU who also studies teamwork, has been doing work on how groups most effectively tap into their collective intelligence in order to do better work as a team. Her studies have shown that groups are able to work better if all the members of the team make equal contributions to discussions and decisions. This dynamic is more likely to happen when the team members are able to empathize with each other and to have an emotional intelligence to infer what their colleagues are thinking or feeling. Interestingly, her studies have shown that teams that have more women on them tend to exhibit these traits more and are better able to tap into the collective intelligence of the group.

5) On ETC Curriculum

- Creative Orchestration
- Master of Entertainment Technology (MET)
- Research & Design
- ETC Projects
- ETC Core Courses
- Learn, Work, Play

CREATIVE CHAOS ORCHESTRATION

What's readily apparent is that the creative process is truly a chaotic experience, and more diversity, while adding challenges, actually helps create better results. To get these positive results, people need to feel included. This is collaborative innovation in practice and process. The ETC faculty are well aware that failures and conflict will most likely occur during a project, so we work to provide teams with support to best orchestrate how they learn, work and play together.

MASTER OF ENTERTAINMENT TECHNOLOGY (MET)

The structure of the curriculum provides the context within which the faculty orchestrates our support for students learning the creative process. The ETC is a two-year professional degree, and students graduate with a Master of Entertainment Technology (MET). A MET is a unique degree that helps us articulate what we're not as much as what we are. For instance, if students are interested in just taking standard technical courses, they'd be better off pursuing a master of science (MS) degree. If students are interested in working on their individual art projects and portfolio, they should pursue a master of fine arts degree (MFA). Similarly, if they're more interested in writing papers than hands-on project, they could consider a master of arts (MA). While students more interested in business should look to a master of business administration (MBA). The MET is similar to a MBA degree in that there is a strong professional focus, but while a MBA concentrates on finances and administration, the MET is focused on creative design and development.

The ETC accepts around 75-80 students a year, so the student body is around 150-160 students. To strike the necessary interdisciplinary balance, we work to recruit 40% of the incoming students out of technical backgrounds (e.g. computer science and engineering) and 40% out artistic backgrounds (e.g. 2D/3D, graphics, UX, visual effects), with the remaining 20% coming from a variety of areas (e.g. theatre, creative writing, industrial design, business, audio, music, communications, etc.). We work to have this mix of students in order to ensure that they can be on interdisciplinary teams throughout their studies. To support the students, we also need to have a diverse faculty and staff with a variety of backgrounds and experiences. This helps all the teams and students have faculty and staff available to support their educational needs and goals. We have students with various interests ranging from technical, artistic, design, audio and production. We also have students interested in industry jobs, or entrepreneurial opportunities, or in furthering their education.

Students are engaged in our project-based curriculum in which they own their intellectual property as they get real-world hands-on experience in design and development. Faculty and staff advise students on both their educational goals and professional aspirations. Within this curricular context, we have found that space is extremely important to the success of projects. Each team shares a large office room where they sit together through their project work. We are also technologically agnostic, in that we do not work to teach specific tools. Instead, we focus on teaching the concepts and processes so that students can adapt and learn to whatever tools they need to use for the project on which they're working.

RESEARCH & DESIGN

The breadth of our interests is one of the strongest components of the ETC experience, so we articulated an applied research and development agenda to help us focus on projects that best innovate across the range of our expertise. This helps us highlight for all involved (students, clients, recruiters, etc.) the type of creative design and development work done at the ETC.

Considering the interdisciplinary nature of the ETC's mission, our overall goal with our project-based curriculum is to provide a context within which students can develop into creative professionals through the process of collaborating on teams working on projects where they have to make things together.

Having worked on these projects, ETC students graduate with two invaluable traits. One, they are fearless about doing something they've never done before. They know they can problem solve together to figure things out. Two, they become leaders and creative professionals who are able to step up collaboratively and take responsibility for their role on a team as well as pushing the envelope on the work being done in the field at large.

ETC project teams work in one of three areas

Transformational Games: including educational games, games for health, games for change, simulations, meaningful gameplay, and in-game assessments, humanities and civics

- to continue iterative rapid-prototyping of games for impact to develop the most effective and impactful games

Innovation by Design: including next-gen interfaces, experimental prototyping, entertainment, creative development best practices, and iterative experience design

- to innovate through development processes and apply the latest technologies to create engaging experiences

Interactive Storytelling: including location-based experiences, mobile, transmedia, augmented reality, and live interactive performance

- to design the most engaging narrative experiences that incorporate multiple media and audience engagement

ETC project teams can focus their overarching goals in one of two ways

Delivery or discovery. Regardless of the focus, the teams must design and develop a final deliverable.

- **Delivery projects** must have a solid, working prototype finished by semester's end.

Constraints become very important on these projects. And a large portion of the evaluation is based upon the quality of the final product in relation to those constraints.

- **Discovery projects** are more open-ended and focus on rigorously exploring ideas through playable proofs-of-concept. And a large portion of the evaluation is on the creative research as it is illustrated through these conceptual proofs.

We are interested in how engagement occurs with different topics, media, groups and contexts regardless of which three areas (Game, Design, Story) and which goal (delivery, discovery) the projects are focused on. We encourage the teams to focus on designing the best experience that the user, player, guest can have.

ETC Projects

Laurie Weingart's study focused on ETC projects, which are the central part of the ETC curriculum. In the project course, students are in small, interdisciplinary teams, creating artifacts under faculty supervision. Artifacts may be software, hardware, illustrated design document, multiple proofs of concept, or a number of these or other things. Artifacts are intended to be prototypes, not production models. Each project team must design what they are going to create, the mechanisms by which they will create it, and then actually create it.

ETC Projects are developed in 3 ways

Client Sponsored: in which an external group supports a project on which an ETC team will work. In the past we have work with companies like: Electronic Arts, Microsoft, Sony, Lockheed Martin, General Motors, Amazon, Bayer, ILM, Intel, Viacom, Legendary, Disney, etc. And we've partnered with non-profit organizations like: Games for Change, Children's Museum of Pittsburgh, Sesame Workshop, Fred Rogers Center, Give Kids the World, Field Museum, Franklin Institute, etc.

ETC Research: in which a faculty member has a research interest on which an ETC team can work. We have had research projects supported by funds from: MacArthur Foundation, Grable Foundation, Benedum Foundation, DARPA, Heinz Endowments, NSF, etc.

Student Pitch: in which a group of students get their pitched project approved by the faculty. Students have pitched projects that have gone on to to be fully developed into a product and serve as the basis of founding a company, like: Experimental Gameplay, World of Goo and 2D Boy, Peacemaker and Impact Games, Digital Dream Labs and Puzzlets, Quasi and Interbots, etc.

All ETC projects must balance two critical issues

Context and process.

- The creation of an environment where all students can receive individual guidance and feedback on how they are doing, in the **context of a group project** where the group succeeding is a paramount value.
- The focus on **process** (learning how to work effectively), **product** (successfully creating an artifact/prototype), and **production** (the team deliverables throughout the semester).

All ETC projects engage in applied design-based research and development where teams apply methodological techniques (rapid-prototyping, iterative design, agile development) to discover fundamental principles (gameplay mechanics, indirect control, interest curves, improvisational storytelling) of how to best design effective interactive experiences.

ETC CORE COURSES

Students start the ETC with a first semester of study that we call "bootcamp," as its goal is to prepare students for the upcoming semester-long projects mentioned above. During this semester, they all take four core courses together: **Building Virtual Worlds (BVW)**, **Visual Story, Improvisational Acting** and the **Fundamentals of the ETC**. This first semester is important in getting them ready to most effectively collaborate on their upcoming projects.

The **Fundamentals of the ETC** provides an overview of the field, with two threads of focus for the course: creative development and professional development. Together, these threads combine to help students start becoming creative professionals who excel in diverse interdisciplinary groups through inclusive teamwork and innovative problem-solving. There are a variety of workshops and seminars throughout the semester, with an overall emphasis on communication and collaboration, challenging students to learn about leadership, teamwork, innovation and positive social impact.

BVW is a rapid-prototyping course where students learn collaborative creative problem-solving. They are placed onto interdisciplinary teams of five, and then they have two weeks to make a virtual reality experience. Then shuffle the teams, two weeks, and make something all over again, and then repeat, for five rounds working with new teams throughout the semester. This course embodies research that suggests that constraints are important. But the structure also highlights the idea that expertise diversity is important, as is adding new voices to a team. BVW implicitly illustrates to our students the importance of constraints and continued attention to inclusive diversity development. The tight timeframes and new teammates each round force students to problem-solve quickly as they work together toward the goals of the rounds.

At the same time students take **Visual Story**, a filmmaking course for non-filmmakers that focuses on how the language of cinema, visuals and audio, can be used to help make experiences more engaging for audiences. In particular, students are learning how to tell stories through visual media. They're also on teams in this course, but they stay on the same team all semester long, so they face different time and team management challenges across the Visual Story and BVW courses.

Finally, students take **Improvisational Acting**, not so that they can become funnier or better actors, but so that they can learn about how share: ideas, space, credit and more. This course helps students develop strategies for creating trust, which research suggests is vital to any diverse interdisciplinary team. Diversity and inclusion don't occur without trust. Once again, the coursework is designed to teach these ideas implicitly, giving students a toolbox for building successful teams. Additionally, improv is a great paradigm for storytelling and collaborative brainstorming with a focus on the importance of the work you're trying to accomplish together. The tenets of improv can helpfully translate to the design and development process, and makes it one of the most important classes for our students.

LEARN, WORK, PLAY

Throughout, the ETC balances educational goals, professional development and engaging experiences; or learn, work and play. We emphasize leadership, innovation and communication by creating challenging experiences through which students learn how to collaborate, experiment and iterate solutions. We challenge and encourage our students to design experiences that educate, engage and inspire.

II. Learning Lessons

II. Learning Lessons

- 6) On Inclusion
- 7) On Collegiality
- 8) On Development
- 9) On Context
- 10) On Support
- 11) On Challenge

Based on Laurie Weingart's study and the faculty's experience with orchestrating support for ETC projects across the years, the second part of the book shares some of the lessons we've been learning as we continue to work on defining best practices. They're clustered into six sections of focus; inclusion, collegiality, development, context, support and challenge.

6) On Inclusion

- Valuing Diversity
- Inclusion, Fit & Diversity
- Improvisational Acting

VALUING DIVERSITY

Saying that we value diversity is easy, but following through on this is important, while also being transparent about what we mean when we say we value it. Diversity is not just in the domain of gender and ethnicity, but also sexual orientation as well as considering socio-economics, culture, religion, age, disability, expertise, work and how the intersectionality of these various categorizations can apply to people, leading to awareness and understanding of the differences amongst a group.

The best way to show that we value diversity is through continually working on being inclusive and supportive where everyone involved feels as if they are part of, and supported by, the group. People need to feel included in order to make this happen. This starts with doing more than just saying it. Both actions and words are important. Saying you value diversity is not enough. You have to follow through on how you actually work together so that everyone on the team feels included.

We firmly believe that being open to diversity enables us to go through the creative process together, which translates into being able to design and develop a greater diversity of products. Noting that this is an ongoing process is important so that we can discuss it together and address it when needed.

Actions and words are how we shape our culture, one in which a community grows together. We work to accept that we're all potentially different, but also that we all can make a difference. This work is not only a process, but also progress, in that we've come a long way, but we still have a way to go. Valuing diversity and being inclusive is a challenge we can face together.

INCLUSION, FIT & DIVERSITY

Considering inclusion, one way to think about it is in terms of fit, how a person feels that they fit within a group, and how the group feels a person fits with them. There are layers to the notion of fitting within a group. At a high level, there's general culture and lifestyle, how a community exists (or not) and the various lifestyles involved. There's also the overarching sense of the field within which this is set and how inclusive and diverse it is in general, which can lead to a sense of being able to have a career within this or that field (or not).

Thinking more specifically, there's the idea of feeling comfortable with the location, where you are in the world, and locales like urban, suburban, and/or more rural settings. Within which you have the actual company and the team you would interact with daily. And last but not least there's the job, and the shared sense of the role and responsibilities.

All of the above plays a part in helping people get a sense of inclusion and belonging within a group and community in general. On top of all of this, people won't necessarily feel included in a group or see how they fit within a community without attention being given on how to enable this to happen. This is particularly true when trying to increase the diversity within a group. Feeling included is easier if everyone is somewhat similar, and a new person fits the mold as it were. The following sections provide some examples and suggestions for ways to help orchestrate support for diverse teams and individuals so that they feel included as part of the group and can collaborate more effectively.

IMPROVISATIONAL ACTING

We often describe improvisational acting (improv), taught by ETC Associate Teaching Professor Brenda Bakker Harger, as the special sauce in our student's graduate studies. We believe improv is one of the most important ingredients that help create an inclusive environment because the "yes, and" nature of supportive sharing during improv encourages participants to play well together. "Yes, and" means that you accept the ideas your fellow participants offer and expand on them, adding new ideas that relate to the experience you're creating together.

This "yes, and" philosophy can be expressed in the three fundamental rules of improvisation that help create a paradigm that all participants need to follow if they are going to work together. The first rule is: Be fun to play with. This is different than being someone who has fun playing. Being fun to play with means having a generous attitude and being willing to share with others and not be too precious with yourself and your ideas. You need to be open and able to listen and incorporate other people's ideas.

The second rule is: Serve the story. In improv, the story is often a scene unfolding in time and space, and participants are encouraged to use a story spine as well as CROW (character, relationship, objective and where) to help in this regard. Serving the story can also apply to anything that a group is working on together. So your focus should always be on the story, or the experience you're trying to create together, rather than your own ideas or agenda.

The third rule is: Make your partner look good. You should focus on helping the people you are working with perform as best they can by supporting them. If your group can all agree to try and enact these rules, you can start to develop trust and respect working with each other. Improv helps participants become more comfortable brainstorming new ideas together, as they work to shape experiences, creating something novel from nothing but their own collaborative creativity.

7) On Collegiality

- People (Can) Suck
- Responsibility
- Comfortability
- Reputation
- Collaboration

PEOPLE (CAN) SUCK

When your goal is to have an inclusive, collegial and collaborative group, you should keep in mind that people (can) suck. Most everyone has the ability to not get along with other people from time to time. This can range from having a bad day, being in a sour mood, generally not being pleasant, and more; not to mention various levels of sexism, racism and other misanthropic tendencies (passive, aggressive or both). Regardless, there will likely be times when your supervisor will suck, or the client, or some of your colleagues. Bureaucracy in and of itself seems to ensure that people can suck. If you've ever been online, you're aware that the public at large can suck. Most important of all, you need to realize that sometimes you can be the one who sucks. Realizing this helps set the stage for how you can pro-actively deal with situations in which people may be sucking.

RESPONSIBILITY

One of the best ways to deal with people's potential to suck, is to step up and take responsibility for things that you can control and effect which can help alleviate stressful situations (both for yourself and for your teammates). While you can't control how others behave, you can own up to the things you can do. You can take responsibility for the work you do as well as for how you deal with your colleagues. You can take responsibility for the mistakes you make, the failures that happen, and the regrets you may have. You should definitely take responsibility for being honest about what you don't know, and being open to learning more. All of the above helps you take responsibility for being your best more often than not.

COMFORTABILITY

Comfortability, while not a word, is a helpful concept to go along with responsibility. Comfortability is a form of confidence grounded in an accommodating ability and ease of associating with others while being your best because you feel comfortable with being responsible for yourself and your actions. As with the improv course, being comfortable with the unknown helps as you will face new challenges, and will have many failures, across your life and career. Finally, you need to be comfortable with yourself. Along with responsibility, developing comfortability can help you thrive in creative, collaborative work as it helps you to be open to the risks and rewards of exploring new ideas together with a group, which enables you do work that is innovative.

REPUTATION

As you work on creative teams, you will develop a reputation with your colleagues. Ideally, you want to become known as a good team member with a positive attitude. You should remember that it's not about how smart or talented you are, nor is it about being better than your teammates. Working to develop trust and respect with each other is a continual process. A simple way to do this is to just be polite and have good manners. The bar is so low you can stand out positively by just being considerate and courteous with others. Students tend to laugh at this assuming that being polite is easy, yet it's remarkable how few people actually do this regularly. If you actually follow through with your actions as well as your words, you are on the path to developing a good reputation.

You should also consider the improv rule of being fun to play with, as opposed to having fun playing. This gets at the idea that the quality of your efforts and work is more important than the quantity. Not every idea is immediately perfect, so you can work together to improve them. Neil Gaiman discusses how professionals can be good, be pleasant, and be on time. Luckily, you really only need to be two of the three. So if you're good and pleasant, people will forgive you if you're late. If you're pleasant and always on time, people will be okay that your work isn't the best. And if you're good and on time, they'll deal with that fact that you're not that pleasant. I also like to think about what you bring to the job; awful – average – awesome. If all you ever do is complain and kvetch, and bring awful to your colleagues, that's what they'll remember. Almost as bad is if you're just regularly average, never really standing out for much of anything one way or the other. Ideally, you bring awesome to the table, where your colleagues have a positive sense of having you as part of the group.

COLLABORATION

When we talk about the design and development process as being collaborative, this extends beyond the immediate team as no project exists in a vacuum. Being at a research university, we often work with external funders and partners on projects with an educational focus. For instance, when trying to make educational video game a fairly standard model of the process tends to start with the funders supporting academics with grants, who then reach out to designers and developers to help make the game, looking to educators as subject-matter experts. Finally we have the students who will be playing the game, getting drenched by all of the good intentions flowing down the steps of this waterfall-like process which is not the best way to really collaborate around a topic and project together.

A better model of collaboration is when you include all of the stakeholders (funders, researchers, developers, educators and learners) throughout the process, which helps instill trust and respect with all involved. This model means you have a much more diverse group of participants, so there's going to be more challenges and conflicts, but also the potential of doing more innovative work together. In some of her other research, Laurie Weingart and Matthew Cronin have explored the importance of groups having mutual trust and respect, where trust is where people believe in each other's honesty, and respect is their regard for each other's values. As they note, trust enables people to rely on each other, and respect helps them to value each other. Together, this helps people feel more included in a diverse group and collaborate together. This model is a co-creative process where the community of people is involved and invested in the work.

8) On Development

- Less Talk, More Rock
- Collaborative Jams
- Playtesting Workshops
- Experience
- Transformational Experiences

LESS TALK, MORE ROCK

Starting with the BVW course, we work to teach students about rapid prototyping to help them develop creative problem-solving skills. One way to describe this is that we encourage less talk, more rock, an idea from Craig Adams, aka Superbrothers. He discusses how Jordan Mechner notes that the classic design process starts first with an inspiration or idea, and then follows with a second step where the group talks about the idea, and finally they go to the third step and start making it, or rocking. Mechner noticed that teams often get bogged down in the talking step, so he recommends they go from the idea step, to the third step, so that they rock more, prototyping their ideas before the discuss them too much. Teams should start prototyping in order to get their ideas into action and are able to see what does or doesn't work. Less talk, more rock.

COLLABORATIVE JAMS

A helpful way to challenge teams to practice rapid-prototyping as they design experiences is to host and encourage participation in game jams and hackathons. Jams and Hackathons are short-term events, usually around 48 hours, where teams form quickly to rapidly prototype a game, gadget or idea. The ETC hosted a "Now I Get It!" transformational 'game' jam in the spring of 2015. This jam was inspired by the "explorable explanations" work Nicky Case and Bret Victor have done that focuses on creating interactive learning experiences as well as the White House Education Game Jam that was held in the fall of 2014 that had teams of jammers as well as educational subject-matter experts. The "Now I Get It!" jam paired development teams with subject-matter experts to collaborate on creating interactive explanations of complex social and educational issues. You can play all the prototypes at: http://nowigetitjam.org. While a jam involves rapid-prototyping, the short timeframe limits what can be accomplished as compared to a semester-long project engagement. One of the things we're currently exploring with jams is to develop a process that starts with a jam, leads to a longer timeframe, like our projects, to create more fully developed prototypes of the most effective jams, and then take even more time to finalize the prototypes that have tested most successfully and develop them into full products.

PLAYTESTING WORKSHOPS

For the creative development process, playtesting is so important to help teams iterate and polish their designs, which we require that they do it. To support them in this regard, we partner with CMU's Human-Computer Interaction Institute (HCII) to offer a series of playtesting workshops. There are various ways to test (e.g. usability testing, focus testing and quality assurance), but playtesting focuses primarily on if your prototypes are creating the experience that you're trying to design. These workshops cover three stages of playtesting.

- Explore: where playtesting helps to explore a design space.
- Refine: where playtesting helps to iterate and refine designs.
- Persuade: where playtesting helps to provide evidence of how the design is working.

The playtesting workshops are meant to help teams make the most of their playtesting and improve their work.

EXPERIENCE

Knowing your design goal is important for the creative development process, and helps a group to critically address their ideas and how they may apply toward the goals. Ultimately, the goal is whatever experience you want the user, player or guest to have when they engage with what you've created. Focusing on the experience ensures that the team is considering the most important part of their design.

Around the ETC there are several concepts that we think help teams focus on the experience that they're working to design. One is the interest curve of the experience. Jesse Schell, ETC Distinguished Professor of the Practice and CEO of Schell Games, discusses how an interest curve is a graphical representation of a player's interest level in a game or experience over the time of their engagement. Considering the interest curve of the experience helps a team to work on the pacing and having the activities escalate toward the goals and end of the experience. Mihaly Csikszentmihalyi's notion of flow, in which a person achieves an optimal experience with a high degree of focus and enjoyment, is another useful way for a team to consider how they're designing the experience. Ian Bogost and Michael Mateas have done work on procedurality as a computational method to express ideas through interactive and emergent experience design. And I've written about three experiential stages or interactivity: involvement, immersion, and investment, that participants go through as they get more engaged in a game or experience. These are just some of the ways to help a team focus on the experience they're designing.

TRANSFORMATIONAL EXPERIENCES

At the ETC, our graduate student project teams are continually creating experiences, and we challenge them to create transformational experiences in which they work to design experiences that will have a positive social impact. Sabrina Culyba, a CMU and ETC alum, is working on a field guide of best design practices for making transformational games that provides an overview for creating experiences with impact in mind. At the ETC, we explore entertainment technologies across the board, and we're interested in how all of these could be used for education and learning, health and medical, civic engagement and more. To encourage students to consider transformational experience design opportunities, the ETC has a Creative Good Fund which enables students to gain experience with real-world non-profit projects at museums, libraries, zoos, arts and human service organizations, etc. The fund helps support students and connects them to non-profits to create work that has a positive impact in the world. We believe you can use your creativity for good, and work to design transformational experiences that can affect positive changes in our daily lives.

Creative Chaos

9) On Context

- Constraints
- Failure
- Doubt
- Curiosity

CONSTRAINTS

Focusing on the experience you're designing helps a team to be more aware of the constraints within which they're working. Creativity needs constraints as a context for a team to do the work. The classic project management triangle of fast, cheap and good, where you often have to trade off and can only get two of the three, helps illustrate the constraints every project faces. So if you want something fast and cheap, it's not going to be good. Or if you want something fast and good, it's not going to be cheap. And if you want something cheap and good, it's not going to be fast. These universal constraints aren't the only ones. Each project has unique constraints based on its own goals. Sometimes you have to say no. While improvisation's "yes, and…" is the epitome of good collaboration, there is also the need to define your constraints. A team can then design toward the project's goals, working to polish their designs. Another project aphorism is that perfect is the enemy of good. In other words, a team needs to design and polish within their constraints in order to finish their project on time and on budget.

FAILURE

A reality of the iterative rapid-prototyping design process is that a team will rarely have the right idea immediately, so they need to become comfortable with testing their ideas, failing, learning from their mistakes and trying again. In order to test their design ideas, teams should playtest their designs with their demographic audience, which will help them determine what is or isn't working. Early rapid prototyping helps a team fail faster as they experiment and explore ideas, problem-solve and iterate toward solutions that meet their project goals.

Ed Catmull, the current president of Pixar Animation Studios and Walt Disney Animation Studios, often discusses the importance of helping teams at Pixar not fear failure so that they feel encouraged to really push and try new ideas. One way that we try to do this at the ETC, is through the First Penguin Award for the Building Virtual Worlds course. This award is bestowed to the team that had the most spectacular failure, shooting for the stars but falling short and burning up on reentry. The award's name comes from the idea that some penguin has to be the first to go into the water, and they may get the reward of all the fish, or the risk of being eaten by a predator. With this award we want to encourage teams to really push themselves, and it also helps us then provide a context for discussing this positive type of failure as opposed to a failure due to a lack of effort.

DOUBT

When a team is iterating on design ideas, they should keep an open mind about what is working or not, and be open to changing their mind. Kathryn Schulz explores how we inherently enjoy feeling that we are right, which can lead us to getting entrenched in our understanding of a situation. Similarly, Jonathan Fields discusses how uncertainty can lead to fear and doubt, but exploring what we don't know is how we can best do innovative work. So, teams should be doubtful of any certainties they may initially have by questioning and challenging themselves. When teams question the answers they receive and challenge their assumptions they are working through the design process to understand what they need to do.

CURIOSITY

Being curious is a great way to remain open to iterating and improving ideas. Australian television journalist Ian Leslie discusses how curiosity is a fundamental drive to explore and understand which helps us to ask open-ended questions as we analyze ideas. You should continually ask questions and engage with what you don't know or understand. Figuring out how stuff works and solving problems leads to lifelong learning as you push into new ideas, topics and areas. Author and Trinity College Professor Barbara Benedict reviews the cultural history of curiosity and how it once was considered a vice as people believed there were things we weren't supposed to know. Through the advances of science curiosity began to be seen as a virtue as we asked questions of the world. Interestingly, in terms of playing games and learning, curiosity can be viewed as cheating as you push at, and sometimes past, the boundaries or constraints within which you're working. Curiosity,

Creative Chaos

expressed through storytelling and model making, helps you make sense of what you're doing, whether it's a project or life in general.

10) On Support

- Difficulty By Design
- Creative Teams
- Feedback
- Criticism & Conflict
- Workshops, Seminars & Concentrations
- Life Long Skills

DIFFICULTY BY DESIGN

As we've said, the creative design process is chaotic and challenging. Design is difficult, so supporting your team and teammates is important. An effective way to do this is to apply design thinking to how you lead and manage a group. Design thinking as a concept was coined by Herbert Simon to define the process through which designers problem-solve and iterate toward solutions. Tom Kelley and Tim Brown, took this notion and applied it at IDEO throughout every level of the business, not just the creative teams. The people that make up any team tend to know when they're engaged in an experience so they can build on that, but you should ask them questions to push them in working to understand that engagement, and in the end you need to let them try design thinking on their own so they can develop the confidence together. You can provide a team context, by shaping their challenges and showing them connections with related work relevant to their project. This support helps teams develop a mastery of their skills as they develop a literacy of expertise in what they're doing when they collaborate through the design process.

CREATIVE TEAMS

Project teams are made up of a diverse group of creative professionals with a variety of skills and expertise. Working through the design process, teams should balance their focus on their group responsibilities and goals that they achieve through their collaborative individual efforts. Chris Bilton discusses the inter-related nature of the management of creativity and creative approaches for management to help understand how we can best to support creativity work in a group. Similarly, Dutch MacDonald and Mickey McManus outline some best practices for forming high-performance creative teams. They focus on the importance of collaboration, trust and environment as key components for developing innovative teams. To help manage this social creative process, you can encourage active life-long learning skills through feedback, critique and training so that teams grow and improve together.

FEEDBACK

Sharing feedback in a constructive manner helps people to improve both individually and together as a group. Randy Pausch said, "When you're screwing up, and nobody is saying anything to you anymore, that means they gave up." Looking at it this way, giving and receiving feedback is a way to show you're committed to your colleagues and their success. Randy would also say that at the ETC we try to give students ten years' worth of feedback during their two years of study. Student project teams get feedback and critique in a variety of ways. First of all, each group is evaluated by the entire faculty on the actual product that they're creating along with how clearly they present this information in written materials and public presentations. These evaluations occur at 1/4s, 1/2s, soft opening and finals during each semester. Following these group evaluations, students have meetings with their project instructors that focus on their individual performance on the team. These meetings help give them a sense of how both they and the group are doing. Outside of the grading, the faculty meets twice a semester around midterms and finals to do a performance review of all the students. If more than half of the faculty have a concern about a student's performance, we collect and share more feedback in order to help them best succeed. Finally, we have public presentations and events where we invite guests to see the student work, which also provides an opportunity to garner even more feedback. Throughout the semester, students are not only getting a lot of feedback, they are getting it from a variety of perspectives; ETC and CMU faculty, their peers and alumni, as well as industry and academic guests. Also, the teams have clear academic goals during their projects, with quick daily meetings, weekly posts to their development blogs and specific milestones that help support them through the design and development process.

CRITICISM & CONFLICT

Giving feedback ideally entails some constructive criticism. We work to help prepare students to both receive and give critique of their work. When receiving criticism, you should to be open (and not immediately defensive and worried about being right) and listen and ask questions to help understand, particularly if the feedback is mixed. Think of criticism as an opportunity to improve the work, which is something you should appreciate. Considering the "yes and.." of improv can help you be open to discussion.

When giving criticism, thinking like a fan, as someone who wants to like the work, can help you to be constructive. You can focus on what works well, then on what you don't understand, and on what you think could make it better. Also, you should make sure to consider the time and place, and if it's in public or should be private, as well as if it's written or verbal or both. Overall, you should keep it short, to the point and focused on the work. Similar to receiving criticism, you should also be open to questions and show appreciation.

Sometimes asking for feedback from others is one of the best ways to get some critical input on your performance that you otherwise might not receive. When asking for feedback, you should be clear that you are looking for honest input and you should be open to hearing what gets shared. You can help focus the feedback by asking for input on three things: what your colleagues appreciate about what you are doing, what they would like you to start doing, and what they would like you to stop doing. This can help lead to a fruitful discussion on what you're doing well and how you can improve.

Of course, you should remember that sometimes the good intentions of sharing feedback can go astray and lead to conflict. To help this be a constructive discussion, as opposed to disruptive argument, you should step back and take some time. Then you should focus on making a resolution as opposed to being right, so that you can move forward.

Along with criticism, sharing praise is also important. As with criticism, when you share praise you should focus on the work and what you appreciate. And when you receive praise you should be thankful and share it around (and don't expect praise for just showing up).

With both criticism and praise, you're sharing feedback to help improve the work. Feedback can happen both informally and formally. In formal critiques, you could consider following Liz Lerman's Critical Response Process. This process starts with statements of meaning by the team or person who is receiving the critique, which helps them articulate what they are trying to do. They follow this by asking questions that they'd like to have answered by the reviewers to help start the discussion. The reviewers can then ask questions that should be initially neutral in evaluation, to help explore their understanding of the work being critiqued. Finally, the team or person can invite opinions from the reviewers based on the overall discussion. The above are just some of the many ways you can work to ensure that criticism can be supportive and disagreements can be constructive, both of which helps a team develop trust and respect and the ability to collaborate well as a team.

WORKSHOPS, SEMINARS & CONCENTRATIONS

Along with the feedback we work to share at the ETC, we also offer multiple extracurricular workshops and seminars to help students develop skills individually and as teams. Providing these opportunities can be an effective way to support the group as a whole by offering a range of topics across a variety of applicable areas. We are continually working to make sure the topics offered are relevant and helpful. They are loosely organized into two groups with one focusing on creative development (Aesthetics, Design, Skills, Process, Playtesting, Critique, Analysis, Project Management, Agile Development, Producing, Storytelling, Life-Long Learning, etc.) and the other focusing on professional development (Strengths, Intellectual Property, Branding, Entrepreneurialism, Conflict Management, Public Speaking, Pitching, Interviews, Professional Communication, Portfolios, Resumes, Personal Health, Field Overview, Professional Development, etc.). These workshops and seminars are meant to complement and support their projects and full courses to help them learn how to become creative professionals.

On top of this, we also offer graduate concentrations in game design, themed entertainment and interactive storytelling, which enable students to focus their elective courses. These concentrations are analogous to more focused creative training and professional certification. We offer these in order to further support students in developing their skills and expertise.

LIFE LONG SKILLS

In the end, the hope is that you can support team members in the development of life-long skills as they become creative professionals. These skills will serve them well in almost any group, team or job in any field. They range from collaboration and cooperation, to communication and attitude, to problem-solving and adaptability to change as well as leadership and management. Finally, the mindsets of creativity and curiosity are important. All of the above can help teams as they work to design and develop engaging experiences.

11) On Challenge

- Hard Fun
- Pleasantly Frustrating
- Challenge Is Good
- Challenge Is Engaging
- Curiosity Literacy

HARD FUN

Seymour Papert and Alan Kay both used the term, "hard fun," to describe activities that are challenging and enjoyable. Similar to the notion of "flow", hard fun is an apt way to consider the collaborative creative design process as well. Ideally, you'd like teams to find the process to be pleasantly frustrating as they're working on interesting design challenges that keep them engaged with their collaborative tasks. The difficulty of the process can lead to more mastery in working together. When team members have the agency to make choices and decisions together, they will become literate in the design process together. Patrick Bateson and Paul Martin explore the importance of openness and playfulness in creativity and developing innovative ideas. This transformational process happens with a project as it starts with diverse group of people who across their time of collaborating form a sense of an inclusive community and culture as they play, learn and create together.

PLEASANTLY FRUSTRATING

James Paul Gee coined the term "pleasantly frustrating" to talk about games that are well designed so that the challenges are balanced across the game to be on a level of difficulty achievable by the player while also ramping up the challenges to meet their abilities as they learn how to play the game better as they progress through it. Jerome Bruner's concept of "instruction scaffolding" in which students are provided with support to help them develop into autonomous learners across time is a similar idea. You can work to help ensure that development challenges fall into the realm of a pleasantly frustrating flow, in which teams aren't faced with tasks that are too simple where they would then start to become bored with the process, nor too hard where they'd get overly stressed by the process. With pleasantly frustrating challenges, people and teams feel capable of learning what they need to do in order to succeed. Of course, in the development process it can sometimes be difficult to ensure that challenges are pleasantly frustrating, but considering them from this perspective can help you support and encourage a team to learn how to solve the challenges together.

CHALLENGE IS GOOD

In thinking about group culture, you should remember that it's not just about having fun together. Fun has a quick half-life and wears off as a primary part of engagement. Raph

Koster talks about fun as a reward to encourage us to learn and explore the possibility space of a game, and a game becomes less fun as we more fully discover all the possibilities of the space. Similarly, Chris Crawford discusses how fun games have smooth learning curves in which a player is enabled to advance through the game as they improve. In both cases, fun is about learning and being challenged. Considering creative design, the difficulty of the challenges that teams have to settle helps them learn to become better at solving problems together as a collaborative group.

CHALLENGE IS ENGAGING

Challenges can be engaging when striking a balance where teams are able to tackle tasks of increasing difficulty as their experience and expertise develops. Greg Costikyan discusses how games inherently involve sets of challenges that keep the player engaged. Similarly, teams having challenges that meet teams at their level of mastery is powerfully engaging. Daniel Pink includes mastery as one of the three elements, along with autonomy and purpose, that are motivating to people and teams. Mastery is the sense that you are getting better at what you do. Autonomy is when you have some control over your work and how you do it. And purpose comes through feeling connected to a cause larger than yourself. Like challenging our students to create transformational experiences, having a strong sense of agency to tackle challenges and exceed expectations is engaging.

CURIOSITY LITERACY

Another important factor in helping teams stay motivated across time is helping the members to develop a curiosity literacy. By this, we mean that team members should work to understand how they learn, and they should be encouraged to grow as creative professionals and begin to address their own challenges. Paul Paulus and Bernard Nijstad explore how innovation can occur through collaboration by enabling the social factors involved in groups doing creative work. Along these lines, Sina Najafi highlights how

Creative Chaos

Cabinet Magazine continually explores curiosity as an ethical imperative to engage with our world and imagine how it might be better. A curiosity literacy entails an active stance that helps people and teams address the life-long challenges of improving what they do and questioning why they do it.

In Conclusion

- Orchestrating Creativity
- More Inclusive Diversity Please
- Creative Chaos
- Learning Lessons
- References

ORCHESTRATING CREATIVITY

While the creative process is chaotic, the ETC continually works to help orchestrate the creativity of collaborative teams so that they can regularly do more innovative work. Through our project-based curriculum and modeling of supportive leadership, we strive to inspire our students and alums to value and embrace inclusive diversity, where people feel a part of a group of creative problem solvers, who are open to improve themselves and their teams, and are comfortable doing things they've never done before.

MORE INCLUSIVE DIVERSITY PLEASE

In closing, we'd like to put out a call for more inclusive diversity please. Not only in the creative fields and entertainment industries, but also across all areas of work and culture. We strongly believe that education leads people to value and embrace inclusive diversity, and that more diversity on teams leads to more diversity in the products they make, and to more creativity in the work they do together. Inclusive diversity is important and valuable, and we have to do it together as we work to make more magic and change the world for the better.

CREATIVE CHAOS

Creative Chaos denotes how the design process is inherently challenging, and having more diverse teams adds to the challenge, but can also spark more creative work. Inclusion leads to innovation as teams learn to collaborate with each other, but the creative design process requires supportive orchestration in order for teams to regularly make the magic.

LEARNING LESSONS

Throughout this book on our thoughts about creative chaos, inclusion and innovation, we have been sharing the lessons we've been learning across the years. We view the experience and expertise we've been developing as "learning lessons" instead of "lessons learned" as it's a continual on-going process in which we always work to make changes and improvements to discover our best practices and break our bad habits. In fact, with the release of this book, we're currently planning more studies to explore this even further, and we will continue to share the lessons we learn. This is the ETC's overarching "yes, and…" approach to learning how to best teach creativity and an inclusive collaborative design and development process.

In Conclusion

This open approach is how we balance educational goals, professional development and engaging experiences as our student teams learn, work and play together. It is why we believe the ETC is different and successful in how we educate, engage and inspire.

References

PREFACE & ACKNOWLEDGMENTS

Davidson, D. "Slides." http://waxebb.com/slides/

ETC. "Alumni." http://www.etc.cmu.edu/learn/alumni/

ETC. "Creative Chaos." http://www.etc.cmu.edu/play/creative-chaos/

ETC. "Faculty & Staff." http://www.etc.cmu.edu/learn/faculty-staff/

CREATIVE CHAOS

ETC. "M.E.T. Curriculum." http://www.etc.cmu.edu/learn/curriculum/

Twain, M. (1998). *The Wit and Wisdom of Mark Twain*. Mineola, NY: Dover Publications.

1) ON THE ETC

Pausch, R. "Randy Pausch." http://www.cs.cmu.edu/~pausch/Randy/oldRandyPage.html

References

2) ON CREATIVITY

Disney Book Group. (1998). *Walt Disney Imagineering: A Behind the Dreams Look at Making the Magic Real*. Anaheim, CA: Disney Editions.

ETC. "Creative Chaos." http://www.etc.cmu.edu/play/creative-chaos/

3) ON ETC RESEARCH

Goh, K., Goodman, P., & Weingart, L. (2013). "Team innovation processes: An Examination of activity cycles in creative project teams." Small Group Research, 44, 159-194.

Todorova, G. (2013). Both cognition and emotions: Disentangling the mechanisms of the conflict-creativity link in diverse innovation teams. Presented at Academy of Management Conference 2013, Orlando, Florida.

Todorova, G., Weingart, L. R., Goh, K., Mayo, A. (2016). Process conflict, idea integration, and process representational gaps in diverse innovation teams. Paper presented as a part of a Showcase Symposium at the Academy of Management Conference 2016, Anaheim, CA.

Todorova, G., Goh, K., Mayo, A., & Weingart, L. R. (2015). A structural approach to idea integration in cross-functional teams. Presented at the 10th annual conference of the Interdisciplinary Network for Group Research (INGroup), Pittsburgh, PA.

Weingart, L., Todorova, G., & Goh, K. (2013). "Conflict Resolution as a Moderator versus Mediator of the Effects of Task, Process, and Relationship Conflict on Team Outcomes." Eighth Annual Interdisciplinary Network Group Research (INGRoup) Conference. Atlanta, GA.

4) ON CREATIVITY RESEARCH

Nelson, B. (2014). "The Data on Diversity." Communications of the ACM. Vol.57, No.11. http://cacm.acm.org/magazines/2014/11/179827-the-data-on-diversity/

Phillips, K. (2014). "How Diversity Makes Us Smarter." Scientific American. http://www.scientificamerican.com/article/how-diversity-makes-us-smarter/

Woolley, A. http://www.anitawoolley.com

5) ON ETC CURRICULUM

ETC. "M.E.T. Curriculum." http://www.etc.cmu.edu/learn/curriculum/

ETC. "Project Course." http://www.etc.cmu.edu/learn/curriculum/project-course/

6) ON INCLUSION

Bakker Harger, B. (2011). "Improv." in *Tabletop: Analog Game Design*. Pittsburgh, PA: ETC Press.

7) ON COLLEGIALITY

Cronin, M. & Weingart L. (2005). "The Differential Roles of Respect and Trust on Negotiation." IACM 18th Annual Conference. Seville, Spain.

Cronin, M. & Weingart L. (2007). "The Differential Effects of Trust and Respect on Team Conflict." *Conflict in Organizational Groups: New Directions in Theory and Practice*. Chicago, IL. Northwestern University Press.

Gaiman, N. (2013). *Make Good Art*. New York, NY: William Morrow.

Weingart, L., Todorova, G., & Cronin, M. (2008). "Representational Gaps, Team Integration and Team Creativity: The Mediating Roles of Conflict and Coordination." 2008 Academy of Management Meetings, Orlando, FL.

8) ON DEVELOPMENT

Adams, C. & Boyer, B. (2010). "Less Talk, More Rock." http://boingboing.net/features/morerock.html

References

Bogost, I. (2007). *Persuasive Games: The Expressive Power of Videogames*. Cambridge, MA: MIT Press.

Bogost, I. (2007). *Unit Operations: An Approach to Videogame Criticism*. Cambridge MA: The MIT Press.

Case, N. et al. (2014). "Explorable Explorations." http://explorableexplanations.com

Csikszentmihalyi, M. (1991). *Flow: The Psychology of Optimal Experience*. New York, NY: HarperCollins.

Culyba D. & Culyba S. (2015). "Now I Get It! A Transformational 'Game' Jam." Entertainment Technology Center. http://www.nowigetitjam.com

Culyba S. et al. (forthcoming 2017). *Transformational Games: a field guide for design leaders*. Pittsburgh, PA: ETC Press.

Davidson, D. (2003). "Interactivities: From Involvement through Immersion to Investment." http://waxebb.com/writings/interact.html

Deloura, M. (2014). "The White House Education Game Jam." U.S. Department of Education. https://www.whitehouse.gov/blog/2014/10/06/white-house-education-game-jam

ETC. "Creative Good Fund." http://www.etc.cmu.edu/play/creative-good-fund/

Hammer, J., Forlizzi, J. & Christel, M. "Playtesting Workshops." http://playtestingworkshops.com/

Mateas, M. (2005). "Procedural literacy: Educating the new media practitioner." *On The Horizon*, 13(2).

Schell, Jesse. (2008). *The Art of Game Design: A Book of Lenses*. Boca Raton, FL: CRC Press.

Victor, B. (2011). "Explorable Explanations." http://worrydream.com/ExplorableExplanations/

9) ON CONTEXT

Benedict, B. (2001). *Curiosity: A Cultural History of Early Modern Inquiry*. Chicago, IL: University of Chicago Press.

Catmull, E. (2014). *Creativity, Inc*. New York, NY: Random House.

Fields, J. (2011). *Uncertainty: Turning Fear and Doubt into Fuel for Brilliance*. London, UK: Portfolio.

Leslie, I. (2014). *Curious: The Desire to Know and Why Your Future Depends on It*. New York, NY: Basic Books.

Schulz, K. (2010). *Being Wrong*. New York, NY: Ecco.

Wikipedia. "Project Management Triangle." https://en.wikipedia.org/wiki/Project_management_triangle/

10) ON SUPPORT

Bilton, N. (2006). *Management and Creativity*. Hoboken, NJ: Wiley-Blackwell.

Brown, T. (2009). *Change by Design*. New York, NY: Harper Business.

Kelley, T. (2001). *The Art of Innovation*. New York, NY: Crown Business.

Lerman, L. (2003). *Critical Response Process*. New York, NY: Liz Lerman Dance Exchange.

MacDonald, D. & McManus, M. (2016). "Building High-Performance Teams for Collaborative Innovation." http://maya.com/content/5-blog/93-a-guide-to-building-high-performance-teamspart-1-evangelize-collaboration/buildinghighperformanceteams.pdf

Pausch, R. & Zaslow J. (2008). *The Last Lecture*. New York: Hyperion.

Simon, H. (1996). *The Sciences of the Artificial. 3rd Edition*. Cambridge, MA: MIT Press.

References

11) ON CHALLENGE

Bateson, P. & Martin P. (2013). *Play, Playfulness, Creativity and Innovation.* Cambridge, UK: Cambridge University Press.

Costikyan, G. (1994). "I Have No Words & I Must Design." http://www.costik.com/nowords.html

Crawford, C. (1984). *The Art of Computer Game Design.* Osborne McGraw-Hill.

Gee, J.P. (2007). *What Video Games Have to Teach Us About Learning and Literacy.* New York, NY: St. Martin's Griffin.

Kay, A & Disney, R. (2003). "Interview with Alan Kay". ACM Computers in Entertainment. Vol.1, No.1. https://cie.acm.org/articles/interview-with-alan-kay/

Koster, R. (2013). *A Theory of Fun.* Sebastopol, CA: O'Reilly Media.

Najafi, S. (2012). *Curiosity and Method: Ten Years of Cabinet Magazine.* New York, NY: Cabinet Books.

Papert, S. (2002). "Hard Fun." http://www.papert.org/articles/HardFun.html

Paulus, P. & Nijstad B. (2003). *Group Creativity: Innovation through Collaboration.* Oxford, UK: Oxford University Press.

Pink, D. (2011). *Drive: The Surprising Truth About What Motivates Us.* New York, NY: Riverhead Books.

Wood, D. J., Bruner, J. S., & Ross, G. (1976). "The role of tutoring in problem solving." *Journal of Child Psychiatry and Psychology*, 17(2), 89-100.

IN CONCLUSION

ETC. "Mission." http://www.etc.cmu.edu/learn/mission/

About the Author(s)

The process of creating this book exemplified creative collaboration. As mentioned in the Preface & Acknowledgments, this book was adapted from talks which were inspired by research on how the ETC teaches collaborative creativity and inclusive innovation. While Drew Davidson compiled the information together, everyone involved contributed to the effort of making this into a book. You can follow the links below to learn more about us.

Drew Davidson. http://waxebb.com/
Laurie Weingart. http://tepper.cmu.edu/our-faculty-and-research/about-our-faculty/faculty-profiles/weingart/weingart-laurie/
Kenneth Goh. http://www.ivey.uwo.ca/faculty/directory/kenneth-goh/
Gergana Todorova. http://bus.miami.edu/faculty-and-research/faculty-directory/management/todorova/
Anna Mayo. http://tepper.cmu.edu/prospective-students/phd/program/organizational-behavior-and-theory/
Dulce Pacheco. http://www.m-iti.org/people/dulce/
Anita Woolley. http://anitawoolley.com/

About the Author(s)

Jodi Forlizzi. http://jodiforlizzi.com/
Brad King. http://www.thebradking.com/
Mary Flanagan. http://maryflanagan.com/
Steve Audia. http://www.etc.cmu.edu/blog/author/saudia/
Brenda Bakker Harger. http://www.etc.cmu.edu/blog/author/bharger/
John Balash. http://www.etc.cmu.edu/blog/author/jbalash/
Eric Brown. http://www.etc.cmu.edu/blog/author/ericbrown/
Jaehee Cho. http://www.etc.cmu.edu/blog/author/jaeheec/
Mike Christel. http://www.etc.cmu.edu/blog/author/christel/
Ruth Comley. http://www.etc.cmu.edu/blog/author/rcomley/
Tom Corbett. http://www.etc.cmu.edu/blog/author/tcorbett/
Dave Culyba. http://www.etc.cmu.edu/blog/author/dculyba/
John Dessler. http://www.etc.cmu.edu/blog/author/jdessler/
MaryCatherine Dieterle. http://www.etc.cmu.edu/blog/author/mb8f2/
Rhea Flores. http://www.etc.cmu.edu/blog/author/rflores/
Jessica Hammer. http://www.etc.cmu.edu/blog/author/jessicahammer/
Erin Hoffman-John. http://www.etc.cmu.edu/blog/author/erinhoffmanjohn/
Chuck Hoover. http://www.etc.cmu.edu/blog/author/choover/
Heather Kelley. http://www.etc.cmu.edu/blog/author/heatherkelley/
Chris Klug. http://www.etc.cmu.edu/blog/author/gcklug/
Melanie Lam. http://www.etc.cmu.edu/blog/author/mjyee/
Stone Librande. http://www.etc.cmu.edu/blog/author/stonelibrande/
Rebecca Lombardi. http://www.etc.cmu.edu/blog/author/rl3j/
Marti Louw. http://www.etc.cmu.edu/blog/author/mrlouw/
Bryan Maher. http://www.etc.cmu.edu/blog/author/bm3n2/
Cari Marty. http://www.etc.cmu.edu/blog/author/cmarty/
Janice Metz. http://www.etc.cmu.edu/blog/author/jmetz/

About the Author(s)

Anita Nebiolo. http://www.etc.cmu.edu/blog/author/anitanebiolo/
Vicki Poklemba. http://www.etc.cmu.edu/blog/author/vp01/
Dave Purta. http://www.etc.cmu.edu/blog/author/dp1m/
Carl Rosendahl. http://www.etc.cmu.edu/blog/author/carlrosendahl/
Shirley Saldamarco. http://www.etc.cmu.edu/blog/author/shirley/
Jesse Schell. http://www.etc.cmu.edu/blog/author/jschell/
Valerie Sofranko. http://www.etc.cmu.edu/blog/author/valeriesofranko/
Scott Stevens. http://www.etc.cmu.edu/blog/author/ss8s/
Susan Timko. http://www.etc.cmu.edu/blog/author/stimko/
Jess Trybus. http://www.etc.cmu.edu/blog/author/jtrybus/
Jon Underwood. http://www.etc.cmu.edu/blog/author/junderwo/
Ralph Vituccio. http://www.etc.cmu.edu/blog/author/rv0a/
Ricardo Washington. http://www.etc.cmu.edu/blog/author/rwashing/
Shirley Yee. http://www.etc.cmu.edu/blog/author/syee/
Caitlin Zunic. http://www.etc.cmu.edu/blog/author/caz/
ETC Alumni. http://www.etc.cmu.edu/learn/alumni/

About the ETC Press

ETC Press is a publishing imprint with a twist. We publish books, but we're also interested in the participatory future of content creation across multiple media. We are an academic, open source, multimedia, publishing imprint affiliated with the Entertainment Technology Center (ETC) at Carnegie Mellon University (CMU) and in partnership with Lulu.com. ETC Press has an affiliation with the Institute for the Future of the Book and MediaCommons, sharing in the exploration of the evolution of discourse. ETC Press also has an agreement with the Association for Computing Machinery (ACM) to place ETC Press publications in the ACM Digital Library.

ETC Press publications will focus on issues revolving around entertainment technologies as they are applied across a variety of fields. We are looking to develop a range of texts and media that are innovative and insightful. We are interested in creating projects with Sophie and with In Media Res, and we will accept submissions and publish work in a variety of media (textual, electronic, digital, etc.), and we work with The Game Crafter to produce tabletop games.

Authors publishing with ETC Press retain ownership of their intellectual property. ETC Press publishes a version of the text with author permission and ETC Press publications will be released under one of two Creative Commons licenses:

- **Attribution-NoDerivativeWorks-NonCommercial:** This license allows for published works to remain intact, but versions can be created.
- **Attribution-NonCommercial-ShareAlike:** This license allows for authors to retain editorial control of their creations while also encouraging readers to collaboratively rewrite content.

Every text is available for free download, and we price our titles as inexpensively as possible, because we want people to have access to them. We're most interested in the sharing and spreading of ideas.

This is definitely an experiment in the notion of publishing, and we invite people to participate. We are exploring what it means to "publish" across multiple media and multiple versions. We believe this is the future of publication, bridging virtual and physical media with fluid versions of publications as well as enabling the creative blurring of what constitutes reading and writing.

http://press.etc.cmu.edu/